Fin Mac Cool

re-told by
Philip Page

Published in association with
The Basic Skills Agency

Hodder & Stoughton

A MEMBER OF THE HODDER HEADLINE GROUP

Acknowledgements
Cover: Doug Lewis
Illustrations: Philip Page

Orders: please contact Bookpoint Ltd, 78 Milton Park, Abingdon, Oxon OX14 4TD. Telephone: (44) 01235 827720, Fax: (44) 01235 400454. Lines are open from 9.00–6.00, Monday to Saturday, with a 24 hour message answering service. Email address: orders@bookpoint.co.uk

British Library Cataloguing in Publication Data
A catalogue record for this title is available from The British Library

ISBN 0 340 80011 9

First published 2001
Impression number   10 9 8 7 6 5 4 3 2 1
Year   2007 2006 2005 2004 2003 2002 2001

Copyright © 2001 Philip Page

Typeset by SX Composing DTP, Rayleigh, Essex.
Printed in Great Britain for Hodder & Stoughton Educational, a division of Hodder Headline Plc, 338 Euston Road, London NW1 3BH by Athenaeum Press, Gateshead, Tyne and Wear.

Finn Mac Cool

Contents

1

The Fianna

The morning mist cleared slowly.
A pale sun rose over the green fields
of Ireland.
It shone on the swords and spears
of two great armies.
Soon, they would fight a terrible battle.

All the warriors were members of the Fianna.
They were soldiers who protected
the High King of Ireland.

They fought against his enemies.
They kept the peace in the land.
But now two of their leaders had fallen out.

The chief of one army was called Cumhail.
He was the leader of the Fianna.
The chief of the other army
wanted to take his place.
His name was Goll.
Their warriors were fierce and brave.
They all knew this would be a battle
to the death.
There could only be one chief of the Fianna!

Cumhail was worried.
He had been told that he would lose
the first battle he fought
after he got married.
Earlier that year he had got married!

Cumhail put that thought out of his head.
He lifted his great, shining sword.
'Charge!' he yelled to his men.
At the same time, Goll's army attacked.

Many men died.
Goll was blinded in one eye.
Cumhail was badly wounded.
Then he was killed by Goll.

Goll cut off Cumhail's head.
He had won the battle.
He was now the leader of the Fianna!

2

Finn's Childhood

While the battle was going on
Cumhail's wife gave birth to a baby boy.
Soon after, a messenger came.
He told her that her husband had been killed.

She looked at her baby.
'They will want to kill you now,' she
whispered to him. 'We must hide you.'

She gave the boy to her two
most trusted women friends.
They promised to look after him well.

The women took the baby into a forest.
There they found a great oak tree.
They carved a room inside the tree.
That was where they lived.
Nobody could find them.

One of the women was a priestess.
The other was a great female warrior.
Together, they taught the boy all they knew.

They gave him a dog to be his friend.
It was called Bran.
It went everywhere with the boy.
It understood every word he said.

The two women and the boy
could never say who he was.
They could not even say his name.
If his enemies knew
he was the son of Cumhail,
he would be killed.
He became known as Finn.
This meant 'the fair-haired one',
because he had blond hair.

Finn learned the ways of the forest.
He knew all the plants and trees.
He knew all the animals, fish and birds.
He grew strong.
He could run as fast as the wind.
He could fight with both spear and sword.

'When you are ready, you must go
to the High King,' the women told Finn.
'You will become the leader of the Fianna.'

'I am ready now,' said Finn.
The two women laughed.

'It takes more than fighting to be a member
of the Fianna!' they said.
'Every warrior is a poet as well.'
'Teach me,' said Finn.

'We have taught you much,' said the women,
'but we cannot teach you the poems
and songs of Ireland's past.'

'Who can?' Finn asked.

'A man called Finegas,' they replied.
'You must go to live with him
and learn from him now.'

3

The Salmon of Knowledge

And so Finn went to stay with Finegas.

The old man taught Finn poems and songs
about Ireland's past.
He learned about giants and heroes,
great battles and brave deeds.
In time he made up his own poems and songs.
They were as good as anything
Finegas had taught him.

Finn noticed that the old man spent a lot of
time fishing in a nearby pool.
He caught lots of fish but
always threw them back.

Then one day he caught a great salmon.
Finn noticed that he was very happy.
He gave it to Finn.
'I want you to cook this for me,' he said.
'But you must not eat any of it.'

Finn agreed.
He built a fire to roast the salmon.
While it was cooking he touched it
and burned his thumb.
He put his thumb in his mouth and sucked it.
A strange feeling came over him.

He told Finegas what had happened.
The old man smiled.
'Ah,' he said. 'I knew the fish
was not meant for me.'

He told Finn that it was a magical fish –
the Salmon of Knowledge.
'Do you see that hazel tree
by the pond?' he said.
'The hazel nuts fall into the water
and the salmon eats them.'

He went on to say that each hazel nut
contained knowledge.
The more the salmon ate,
the more knowledge it got.

'Now you have the salmon's knowledge
in your thumb,' he told Finn.
'Every time you suck your thumb,
you will be able to use that knowledge
to solve your problems.'

'I have taught you all I can,'
he said to Finn.
'Now you must go to the High King
at the Hill of Tara.
You are ready to take your place
as leader of the Fianna.'

4

Tara

Finn set off.
He took Bran with him.
It took him many days to reach Tara.

He looked at the hill.
He was amazed!
He saw old standing stones.
He saw great wooden halls.
But the buildings seemed to be so new.

Guards stopped him when he came close.
'What do you want?' they asked him.
'I have come to see Cormac,
the High King of Ireland,' he said.

'What is your name?' they said.
'What do you want?'
'I will tell that to Cormac,' Finn replied.

They would not take him to the king.
The weeks passed.
The leaves began to fall from the trees.

Finn noticed that everybody
seemed to grow nervous.
'What is the matter?'
he asked one of the soldiers.

'Tomorrow is the great autumn feast of
Samhain,' the soldier said.
'It will be a time of great sorrow.'

He told Finn what would happen.
Every year at this time an evil goblin
came to Tara.
It played magic music to everybody there.

It made them all fall asleep.
Then the goblin breathed fire.
It burned all the buildings down.

Finn sucked his thumb.
He knew what to do.

He found a man with a magic spear.
The man had been a friend of his father.

'Take the spear,' said the man.
'Press it against your cheek
when the goblin sings.
Then you will not fall asleep.'

That night Finn waited.
He heard the sound of beautiful music.
It came from the forest.
He looked at the people near to him.
Their eyes began to close.
Their heads dropped.
They began to fall asleep.

Finn pressed the spear against his cheek.
He saw the goblin coming.
He saw it breathing fire from its mouth.

Bran was by his side.
The dog jumped up and attacked the goblin.
Then Finn threw the spear.

It hit the goblin in the chest.
The goblin fell to the ground.
Finn drew his sword and cut off its head.
Tara was saved!

Cormac, the High King of Ireland,
sent for Finn.
He thanked him and asked him who he was.

'I am Finn Mac Cool,' said Finn.
'My father was Cumhail,
Chief of the Fianna.'

'What do you want?' asked the High King.

'I have come to claim my father's place as
chief of the Fianna,' said Finn boldly.

Cormac looked about the great hall.
'This young man has proved his bravery,'
he said. 'Will any man challenge him?'

Goll of the One Eye stepped forward.

'I killed your father,' he said.
'Will you now kill me?'

'No,' said Finn.
'You killed my father in battle.
It was a fair fight.'

Goll nodded.

'There is no place in the Fianna for revenge,'
Finn said.
'There is only a place for great warriors!'

Everybody in the great hall cheered.

'I can think of no better man to lead the
Fianna,' said Cormac. 'Let it be so.'

5

The Magic Deer

Finn led the Fianna well.
He was fair and strong.
He was a great fighter in battle.
For many years there was peace in Ireland.

One day Finn went hunting.
He saw a beautiful young deer.
He sent Bran and his other dogs after it.

The dogs caught the deer
but did not attack it.
Finn thought this was strange.
He did not kill the deer.
He left it in the forest
but it followed him home.

When they came to his hall, the deer changed
into a beautiful young woman.
Finn was amazed!

'My name is Saba,' said the woman.
'A wizard turned me into a deer
because I would not marry him.'

'Stay with me and you will be safe,'
said Finn.
'His magic will not harm you here.'

Finn and Saba were married.
They were very happy together.

Then one day Finn was called away.
The Fianna had to fight against
some invaders.
Saba watched and waited every day for him
to come back.

When she saw him she ran out to meet him.
But it was not Finn.
It was the wizard!
He had cast a spell
to make him look like Finn.

Saba was changed back into a deer.
The wizard took her far away.

Finn searched for his wife for seven years.
He never found her.
But he did find a small boy in the forest.
He sucked his thumb.
He knew it was his and Saba's son.
Finn called him Oisin, which means
'Little Deer'.

6

Grainne and Diarmuid

The Fianna grew stronger as Finn grew older.
When he was an old man,
the High King sent for him.

'I want you to marry my daughter, Grainne,'
he said to Finn.
'That will make the friendship between us
even stronger.'

Finn was pleased, for Grainne
was a beautiful young woman.

But Grainne did not love Finn.
She loved a younger warrior in the Fianna.
His name was Diarmuid.

The king gave a great feast to celebrate the
engagement of Grainne and Finn.
But that night, when everybody was asleep,
Grainne and Diarmuid ran away together.

Finn was furious.
He chased them all over Ireland.
They could never spend more than
two nights in any place.
They were hunted wherever they went.

At last Finn gave up.
He promised he would not harm them.
Grainne and Diarmuid believed him.
They came back to live in Tara.
But Finn was still angry and jealous!

Finn took Diarmuid hunting one day.
They found a great wild boar.
Finn knew that this boar was very dangerous.

'Are you brave enough to kill that boar
yourself,' he said to Diarmuid,
'or do you want me to help you?'

Diarmuid did not want Finn to think
he was afraid.
With his spear in his hand
he chased the boar.

The boar turned and charged at Diarmuid.
He was thrown from his horse.
The boar wounded him with its sharp tusks.

He called to Finn for help.
'The boar has poison in its tusks,' he gasped.
'Please wash the poison out of my wound.'

Finn went to a stream.
He brought back some water in his hands.
But he was still jealous of Diarmuid.
He let the water slip through his fingers!

Finn Mac Cool had changed.
On that day he lost his honour.

7

The End of the Fianna

Many people did not like the Fianna.
One of them was the High King's son.
His name was Cairbe.

He thought that the Fianna
had become too powerful.
He did not like the way
the High King had to pay
lots of money for them to protect him.

When he became the High King,
he plotted against the Fianna.
Many other chiefs in Ireland joined him.
Among them was Goll of the One Eye!

Cairbe raised a great army.
It outnumbered the Fianna by ten to one.

By now Finn was too old to fight.
The Fianna was led by his son, Oisin,
and his grandson, Oscar.

With their few warriors
they faced Cairbe's mighty army.
The battle lasted all day.

Finn watched from a boat just off the shore.
He saw Oscar kill Cairbe.
Then Oscar was slain.
With tears in his eyes,
Finn saw the end of the Fianna.
Only Oisin and one other man escaped alive!

And Finn?
What happened to him?
Some say that he was killed too.
Some say that he simply faded away.
Others say that he sleeps in an enchanted
cave with the ghosts of the Fianna.
When Ireland needs him – he will awake!